Virtual Mythology

Story by Sarah Fallon

Illustrations by Alessandra Vitelli

Virtual Mythology

Text: Sarah Fallon
Publishers: Tania Mazzeo and Eliza Webb
Series consultant: Amanda Sutera
Hands on Heads Consulting
Editor: Susan Keogh
Project editor: Annabel Smith
Designer: Jess Kelly
Project designer: Danielle Maccarone
Illustrations: Alessandra Vitelli
Production controller: Renee Tome

NovaStar

ISBN 978 0 17 033512 6

Cengage Learning Australia
Level 5, 80 Dorcas Street
Southbank VIC 3006 Australia
Phone: 1300 790 853
Email: aust.nelsonprimary@cengage.com

For learning solutions, visit **cengage.com.au**

Printed in China by 1010 Printing International Ltd
1 2 3 4 5 6 7 29 28 27 26 25

Nelson acknowledges the Traditional Owners and Custodians of the lands of all First Nations Peoples. We pay respect to Elders past and present, and extend that respect to all First Nations Peoples today.

Contents

Chapter 1	Excursion Day	5
Chapter 2	Cognitivia Games	8
Chapter 3	Press Play	12
Chapter 4	The Labours of Herakles	15
Chapter 5	The Nemean Lion	21
Chapter 6	The Augean Stables	25
Chapter 7	Taming Kerberos	32
Chapter 8	The Hind and the Hydra	37
Chapter 9	The Birds	41
Chapter 10	Return to the Hydra	50
Chapter 11	Back at Last	55

ROCK

Chapter 1

Excursion Day

Reggie took off the virtual reality headset and put down the controllers. It was time to go to school, and his mum hadn't needed to pester him even once to stop playing. It had to be a first. Today, Reggie was excited to go to school – it was excursion day. Reggie had been looking forward to it all term. The class was visiting Cognitivia Games, a virtual reality gaming company. Reggie's dad was really into technology, and always had to have the latest gadgets. He'd bought them both headsets for Christmas, and it had been Reggie's dream to be a virtual reality game developer from then on. This school trip was perfect for him.

Reggie practically pounced on his backpack and headed for the door. His mum blinked in surprise. "Someone's keen," she said.

Reggie rolled his eyes. "It's excursion day, Mum."

"Oh, right. Well, enjoy yourself." His mum ruffled his hair.

"Of course I will," Reggie said, swerving out of reach.

Reggie ran out the door and jumped the flower bed that separated their driveway from the Carlsons', their neighbours. After his mum started working from home, Reggie had been driven to school by the Carlsons. The families had lived next door to each other since Reggie was three. He and their son, Oliver, had been born only a week apart and were in the same class at school.

Carpooling just made sense, his mum had said. But Reggie couldn't stand it. Oliver drove him mad. Their parents were best friends and had been enrolling the boys in the same activities since they could walk, and Oliver was always better at them. The only thing Reggie had all to himself was gaming, but Oliver had even been getting into that lately, too. They'd been entering the same school e-sports competitions but, thankfully, Reggie was still coming out on top. It was only a matter of time, though. Oliver was good at everything. He was always reading – whether it was science or history or novels, it didn't matter – and so he knew about everything, too.

Mr Carlson's car was waiting in the driveway with the engine running. The boys slid into the back seat.

“Hey mate,” said Mr Carlson. “Are you as excited for this excursion as Oliver is?”

“You bet he is,” Oliver said, before Reggie had a chance to answer. “Reggie’s the best gamer.”

“It’s not just about the gaming,” Reggie said. “I want to see all the behind-the-scenes stuff too.”

“Oh yeah?” said Mr Carlson as he reversed onto the road.

“Yeah. I’m going to be a VR developer one day.”

“That sounds fun,” replied Mr Carlson.

“I think it’s awesome how virtual reality is a world created by a computer that looks real. It’s so cool that you can interact with it as if you’re really there. I’d love to be the developer who creates it all, just by coding on a computer,” Reggie continued.

“That’d be so good,” Oliver said.

Chapter 2

Cognitivia Games

Reggie could hardly wait to catch his first glimpse of Cognitivia Games.

But it wasn't the big glamorous building he'd been expecting. It turned out Cognitivia Games was a small independent company. Their teacher, Mr Nguyen, called it "indie". The company only occupied one floor of the bland grey skyscraper the class filed into. They took the lifts to level three, where there was a cool "Cognitivia Games" sign that looked like it was made from living plants. On closer inspection, Reggie realised the sign was a projection, just like VR technology but without the headset. That made the sign even cooler. Standing in front of the sign, an employee from the company waited for them.

"Hi," the employee said with a big smile and wave. "I'm Becky. I'll be showing you around the company today."

Mr Nguyen shook her hand and introduced himself.

"Now," said Becky, "does anyone here play video games?"

Almost the whole class raised their hands.

"And has anyone here ever played a virtual reality video game?"

This time, only Reggie raised his hand.

"Great, can you tell your class what it's like?" Becky asked Reggie.

"It's the most amazing thing ever," said Reggie. "You wear a headset and have these controllers you hold in your hands with sensors so you can actually interact with things in the game with your own body." Reggie looked around at the rest of his class. "But sometimes, when I play too long, I get a headache." He glanced at Becky, who was chuckling quietly. Reggie wished he hadn't added that last bit.

"That's actually very common," Becky said. "Which is why we're working on a game-play experience that doesn't require headsets or controllers at all."

Oliver raised his hand and Becky nodded towards him. "How does it work?" he asked.

"It's still in development," Becky said. "So, I'm afraid that's top secret." She held a finger to her lips with a smile. "Cognitivia Games is working on a lot of exciting new developments in VR, but for now, shall we begin the tour?"

Mr Nguyen agreed, and Becky led the class through the glass doors into the office. Reggie still had a million questions. If Oliver hadn't interrupted, he might have had the chance to ask one.

Becky walked everyone around the office space, pointing out different areas and introducing them to lots of people.

"As you'll see, most of our office is open plan," Becky gestured. She then stopped with the class in front of a closed door. "But we do have some closed rooms. These are where we test our latest games and other technologies. Behind this door, for example, is where we are working on the new mode of VR technology I mentioned earlier.

It's more immersive and realistic than ever before." Becky smiled at Reggie. "And with fewer headaches for anyone playing it."

Reggie raised his hand. "Do we get to see it?"

"Afraid not. It's still far too early to share with the public."

Becky started moving on, but Reggie's eyes lingered on the door. Then, the door suddenly opened. Two employees came out. They didn't even see Reggie standing there, and when the door swung shut behind them, Reggie saw that it didn't quite latch. He looked around. The rest of the class had rounded a corner and was out of sight.

Slowly, Reggie pushed thc "open" button on the keypad half-expecting alarm bells to go off. Nothing. Quickly and silently, he slipped through the door.

Chapter 3

Press Play

The room was dim, lit only by the standby lights on the various monitors and other equipment in front of him. Reggie took a step forward and several overhead lights flickered on. Before him was an open space framed by desks with big monitors on top. He walked into the middle of the room. Behind the desks was a digital whiteboard with writing all over it. Reggie went over to read the notes.

- *Bringing to life the five senses – sight, sound, smell, taste and touch.*
- *To do – build "exit" and "save" systems.*

Touch, Reggie thought. Imagine if you could actually feel a virtual reality world around you. That would be so cool. Exit and save systems were pretty important parts of a game. Reggie was always saving his progress when he gamed at home. He didn't want to lose anything if he had to stop playing for guitar practice.

Reggie walked over to a computer and rolled the trackball in the mouse. A screen flickered on. It hadn't been off long enough to go back to the log-in screen, so it immediately showed what the developers had been working on. It was a new game. “The Labours of Herakles” was written as if carved in stone and there was a picture of a shield with a man’s face on it. It reminded Reggie of some of the artefacts at the ancient Greece museum exhibition his parents had dragged him to. Below that was a button that said *Play*.

Reggie hovered the cursor over the button but didn’t click it. He’d love to play the game, but he didn’t think he’d have time. Especially if he couldn’t exit until the game was complete.

Reggie was ready to leave when he heard footsteps. He ducked behind the desk.

“Reggie,” someone whispered.

Reggie peered around the monitor and saw Oliver looking around with a frown.

"What are you doing here?" Reggie snapped, emerging from behind the desk.

Oliver stormed over to him. "What am *I* doing here? What are *you* doing here? We're about to watch a presentation. Mr Nguyen sent me to find you," Oliver said, putting his hand down on the desk and accidentally knocking the mouse off. It landed upside down on the floor. Then a booming voice said, "Game launch." Only it sounded strange, like it was happening inside Reggie's head rather than out in the room.

"What's happening?" Oliver asked.

"You must have pressed *play* when you knocked the mouse. The game's starting," Reggie accused.

"Everything looks weird," said Oliver.

"It's fine," Reggie said. "We're not wearing any headsets; let's just leave."

But Oliver was right. Everything did look weird, sort of blurry. Then Reggie's legs stopped working properly. He couldn't move.

Chapter 4

The Labours of Herakles

The odd sensation that Reggie was rooted to the spot passed and his vision cleared. But he was no longer standing in the off-limits room at Cognitivia Games. He was standing on some kind of elaborate stone porch lined with marble columns. Writing appeared before Reggie's eyes, as if hanging in the sky. It read *The Palace of King Eurystheus*. Once it vanished, he saw a man wearing what looked like an enormous white bed sheet wrapped around his body and a golden band around his head, sitting on a throne, in front of the wall at the back of the porch. The wall was painted with a huge procession of cattle and people; it looked a bit like a rodeo.

Reggie also noticed a young man standing next to him. He was impressively tall, and built like an Olympic weightlifter. He was wearing some kind of kilt. Strangely, for a man that big, Reggie was sure he had a look of panic on his face.

"You have twelve labours to complete, Herakles," the king said suddenly, looking at the man beside Reggie. "Only then can you return whence you came."

Herakles? Labours? Wasn't that the name of the game Reggie had seen on the screen in the off-limits room? He and Oliver hadn't put on any headsets, but then wasn't that what Becky had said? Cognitivia Games was developing new technology. It must be a way of playing without headsets. Reggie couldn't believe what was happening; it seemed so real.

If Reggie hadn't been so worried about getting caught, this would have been the best day of his life. He needed to exit that game now, but how, if there weren't any controllers? Maybe it was voice activated.

“Pause,” Reggie said, but the king kept talking.

“These are your labours, Herakles,” he announced, and then started reading through a list of tasks. Reggie thought they sounded a lot like the tasks that needed to be done to move through the levels in a game, but he couldn’t get caught up with all that; he had to get out of the game.

“Menu,” Reggie said. “Exit. Escape.” Nothing, nothing and nothing.

The Herakles character looked at him, eyes wide. “Reggie?”

Reggie looked him up and down. He looked so real, but his voice was so familiar. “Oliver?”

Reggie finally looked down at his own body, only it wasn’t his own. His arms were thick and muscly, and he was wearing some kind of tunic.

Reggie felt his face and hair. His hair was long and wavy instead of short and straight.

"We're characters in the game, Reggie!" Oliver said, drawing back Reggie's attention. "How do we get out?"

"I don't know. I think ..." Reggie remembered what he'd seen written on the whiteboard. The developers hadn't created a way of saving or exiting the game yet. His stomach dropped. "I think we have to complete the labours to get out."

Panicked, Oliver ran at the king. "We have to get out," he said, grabbing him. He raised the king high above his head, not realising his own strength. The king didn't even react.

Oliver set him back down. "What's wrong with him?"

"He's an NPC," Reggie said, remembering how new Oliver was to gaming. "A non-playable character. They can only say and do what they've been programmed to."

"So we're stuck here?" Oliver snapped.

"No, we can get out, we just have to complete the game first."

As if on cue, the king walked to Oliver with a scroll. "Here is your list of tasks. Complete them and you will be free."

Reggie and Oliver trudged down the steps of the palace porch.

"So, what's the first task?" Reggie asked.

Oliver unfurled the scroll. "Defeat the Nemean lion and return with proof that it has been done."

"Is there a map?" Just as Reggie said the word "map", a map popped up in front of them like a big projector screen. The heading on top of the map read *Ancient Greece*.

"I thought we might be in ancient Greece," Reggie said.

"Yeah," said Oliver. "Herakles is an ancient Greek hero. He's the son of the king of the gods. He's meant to be super strong."

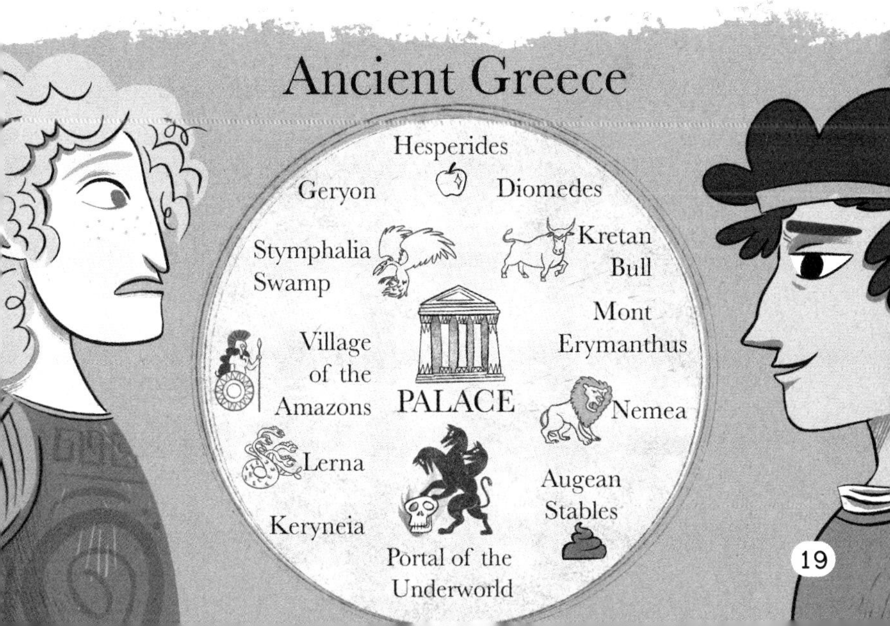

"Great, so you're some super-strong hero, and who am I?" Reggie groaned, gesturing to his unfamiliar body. Of course Oliver would get the cool character.

"Maybe you're another hero, like Perseus," Oliver suggested. "Although ... you're a bit small."

Reggie glared up at Oliver, then stomped off. "Herakles had a sidekick sometimes too; I forget his name," Oliver said, following him.

Reggie didn't like the idea of being Oliver's sidekick at all.

They were just about to pass through the city gates when another NPC approached them. "Hello, Herakles. Hello, Iolaus," the NPC said.

"That was the sidekick's name – Iolaus!" Oliver shouted triumphantly.

Reggie sighed.

The NPC continued, "You'll need these if you hope to succeed in your quests." He handed Oliver a sword and a club, then passed Reggie a bow and a quiver of arrows.

"At least I've got a cool weapon," Reggie said.

Oliver frowned. "I've never played any fighting games before."

Chapter 5

The Nemean Lion

A short while later, Reggie and Oliver arrived at a cave. The writing appeared before their eyes again. This time it read *Nemea*.

"Right, we're here," said Oliver. "So, where's this lion?"

"Probably in there." Reggie nodded at the cave. He drew his bow and notched an arrow.

Watching Reggie, Oliver clumsily pulled out his sword.

The twittering of birds that had surrounded them stopped. After a moment, the silence was filled with a low, rumbling growl. Then the lion emerged from the shadows of the cave. It stood taller even than Herakles, and when the sun hit its body it glinted, as if covered in metal rather than fur.

Oliver took a step back. Reggie pulled on his bow and released an arrow, then quickly notched and released another. Both arrows hit the lion. Both arrows glanced off its glistening fur and lodged in the dirt instead.

"I think it's impenetrable. Try your sword!" Reggie yelled at Oliver.

"Are you joking? I'm not going near that thing!" Just as Oliver got the words out, the lion pounced towards him. He threw the sword to the ground and ran behind a nearby tree.

Reggie dived onto the sword. He came up on his knees and sliced the sword across the lion's chest. There was a resounding clang like metal on metal. Yep, definitely impenetrable, Reggie thought.

The lion pulled back one enormous forepaw and batted Reggie like a ball of wool. Reggie went flying into the tree Oliver was hiding behind and crumpled to the ground. Reggie felt as if he couldn't breathe. His arm stung where the lion's claws had scratched him, and his back and chest burned from the impact of hitting the tree. He was feeling real pain. How could he be feeling real pain inside a *game*? And if he was feeling real pain, was he really injured, too?

Reggie fumbled with his bow. He grabbed an arrow. Perhaps the lion had a weak spot, maybe its mouth. Then, suddenly, Oliver came springing out from behind the tree, club raised high with both hands. He brought it down hard on the lion's head and the creature dropped unconscious.

Reggie scrambled to his feet and picked up his bow. "Great," he puffed. "Now we just need to find its weak spot."

"I don't think we need to kill it," Oliver said. "Just defeat it and bring back proof."

"Okay, so how do we get proof?" Reggie asked.

"We can cut off some of its mane," Oliver said.

"And how are we going to do that? Its whole coat is impenetrable, remember?"

"I reckon we can use the lion's own claws to cut off a chunk. We can take that back to the king as proof," suggested Oliver.

Reggie shrugged. He walked over to the lion and tried to lift up its enormous paw. He could barely get it off the ground. "Well, that's not going to work," he said.

"Let me try," said Oliver, stepping forward. "Super strength, remember?"

Reggie grudgingly stepped aside. Oliver easily lifted the lion's paw and manipulated its claws to cut the mane.

Reggie rubbed the scratch on his arm. It stung. And his chest still hurt when he breathed. He knew he should tell Oliver about his theory that they could really be hurt in the game.

Oliver stood up, holding a chunk of mane and grinning.

Reggie rolled his eyes and decided not to say anything. If Oliver was so smart, he could figure it out for himself.

Chapter 6

The Augean Stables

Just like in other games Reggie had played, you could return to a location you had already been by clicking on it on the map, or, in this case, saying its name out loud. It was a handy shortcut. Reggie and Oliver were able to get back to the palace instantly.

When they climbed the steps of the palace porch and handed the chunk of mane to the king, a flourish of music sounded and writing appeared in the air. It read *Level Complete.*

Oliver pulled the scroll out of his belt. The second labour on the list was to clean the Augean stables.

“How hard could it be?” Oliver said. “My cousins have horses. I’ve helped muck out stables before.” Reggie was just glad it didn’t sound dangerous.

They followed a river marked on the map to where the Augean stables were located. The smell hit them first. “What is *that*?” gasped Reggie. It smelt like a toilet with a plumbing problem – only ten times worse.

“Are you supposed to be able to smell things in virtual reality? How does that work?” Oliver asked, pinching his nose.

“I’ve never come across it before,” Reggie said. He started coughing as they drew closer to the stench. “It must be the VR advancements they’ve been making.”

Once Reggie and Oliver reached the stables, they understood why the smell was so intense. These were nothing like Oliver’s cousin’s stables. Inside them were all kinds of farm animals, not just horses. Animal dung of all different shapes, sizes and odours was spilling out of the stalls and onto the path. No wonder it stank so bad.

Standing at the entrance to the stables was a man in an elaborate outfit just like King Eurystheus. He also had an old-fashioned wooden clothes peg squashed over the end of his nose.

When Reggie and Oliver reached the man, he said, "I am King Augeus. These are my stables,"

"Um, King Eurystheus sent us," said Oliver.

"Wonderful. You must clean out these stables in one day and then your labour will be complete."

"One day!" Oliver exclaimed.

"Here you go," said King Augeus, handing them both shovels. "And you may be wanting these." He held out two clothes pegs.

"Thanks," Reggie snorted. He and Oliver gingerly placed the pegs on their noses.

Inside the stables, mountains of dung rose up around them.

"This is impossible," Oliver said, as he dug his shovel deep into the side of a heap.

“There’s no way we can do this in one day,” Oliver continued. “Even with my super strength.” He flung the poo out the window on a patch of ground with a sign saying *dung heap*. “And if we keep going like this we’re just going to have a dangerously tall tower of poo next to the stables. How is that any better than having mountains of it inside the stables?”

Reggie had been frowning as he moved much smaller shovelfuls of dung outside, barely listening to Oliver. “It must be a puzzle,” he said finally.

“What?” said Oliver, still clearly worked up about the task.

“A puzzle. Even the Nemean lion was a puzzle. Neither task is just about brute strength; there’s a trick to them. Something we have to figure out.” Then, still deep in thought, Reggie slipped om a cowpat.

Oliver burst out laughing.

"You know," Oliver said suddenly, "I noticed the path here has been set lower into the ground than the surrounding land. It almost looks like a dried-up river bed."

"Yeah," said Reggie, getting up and checking just how much of him was covered in poo.

"And there was that big river running outside."

"What are you getting at?" Reggie snapped.

"Well, if we knock out the far wall of the stables and dam up the river, it should divert the water down the path so it runs straight in and out of the stables, washing them clean. You could even grab a quick bath while we're at it." Oliver smirked.

Reggie's eyes narrowed. They had to get out of this game. He couldn't bear another minute with super-strong, super-clever Oliver.

It didn't take Oliver long to knock out the far wall of the stables. After that, they went back to the river. Reggie couldn't believe how obvious it was now. Of course they were supposed to dam it. There were enormous boulders right beside it, clearly designed for the Herakles character to shift. Why hadn't he seen it earlier? He was the gamer here; Oliver was a total newbie.

Oliver picked up the boulders and tossed them into the river with ease, while Reggie watched on uselessly. The water in the river began to rise and, in no time at all, jumped the bank and started to cascade down the path at enormous speed.

Reggie and Oliver raced down beside it and got to the stables just in time to see the poo gush out the other end.

Oliver was beaming. Reggie thought he looked smug, and grudgingly followed him back to the river to remove the boulders. Once the water stopped raging down the road, the music and writing in the air appeared, letting them know the level was complete.

"It must be nice having all that extra Greek myth knowledge," Reggie snarked as Oliver removed the last boulder.

"What do you mean?" Oliver asked.

"Knocking out the lion, flooding the stables. I'm guessing you already know how all the labours are solved, right?"

"No, actually," Oliver said, frowning. "I would have said if I did. I just know who Herakles and some other gods and heroes are because I read a novel they were in. I haven't heard of the labours before."

"Yeah right, then how are you figuring out all the challenges so easily?"

"Oh, I see," said Oliver. "You don't think I could figure them out myself because I haven't been playing video games as long as you have?"

"It's the only thing you weren't great at. Video games were my thing, but you had to start gaming too and now you're better at it than me." Reggie stomped his foot.

"I'm not better. Besides, my parents are always talking about how great you are. It's so annoying," Oliver shouted back. "I'm sick of it. The sooner we get out of here and I can get away from you the better. Let's split the tasks and get them finished *separately*. If you can do them without me."

Reggie snatched the scroll and tore it in half. "Don't come crawling to me when your beginner's luck runs out," he snapped as he turned to walk away.

"Believe me, I won't." Oliver glowered.

Chapter 7

Taming Kerberos

Reggie stormed off into the woods. He couldn't believe Oliver was doing better than him at this game. Well, Reggie was going to prove that he was still the better gamer; he just had to finish his half of the labours first.

Reggie looked at the torn scroll. Taming Kerberos, Guardian of the Underworld, was next. Who or what was Kerberos, Reggie wondered. Oliver might know, but then again, he might not. Maybe he really hadn't known about the lion and the stables, though Reggie doubted it.

"Map," Reggie said, relieved he could still access the map without Oliver there. Marked on the map, not too far away, was *Portal to the Underworld*.

The entrance to the Underworld turned out to be a tunnel in the side of a cliff. Standing outside it was a tall woman, holding two flutes joined in a V-shape. When Reggie approached her, she began to speak.

"This tunnel leads to the Underworld, the land of the dead, where all men fear to tread. To make it safely out again, don't look back, and remember, a pretty tune will soothe the savage beast."

Reggie stepped into the tunnel and his body was enveloped by an icy chill. It was dark except for a dim light in the distance. He walked towards it. At the end of the tunnel was an open cavern lit by beams of sunlight coming through cracks in the rock of the ceiling. As soon as Reggie stepped into the cavern, his body was shaken by an enormous roar. Towering above him was a gigantic, three-headed dog, each head with eyes that burned like coals and jaws dripping with drool. This must be Kerberos, Reggie thought.

The central head dived at Reggie and he quickly jumped away, remembering the pain the lion had inflicted.

Reggie jumped again and again as the other two heads followed the first. Then he spotted a crack in the wall, big enough for him to slip inside but not so big that a giant dog head could. Reggie ran for it, Kerberos's jaws snapping shut behind him. The monstrous beast chomped at the crack a few more times, but it was too narrow. It turned and thumped away.

Reggie inched back closer to the opening to look around. There wasn't much in the cavern besides the dog. There were cracks, just like the one he was hiding in, all along the walls. He was alarmed to see a few skeletons. A couple of the skeletons were holding things: one had a sword and shield and another had a strange instrument that looked a bit like a harp crossed with a guitar.

It made the most sense to go for the sword and shield, but he was supposed to capture the creature, not kill it. Besides, the other two labours had been more puzzling than that. What was it the strange woman had said? A *pretty tune will soothe the savage beast*. Had her flutes been a clue? Maybe he was meant to get the instrument in here.

Of course, the instrument was further away from Reggie and right beside the terrifying monster. But the sword and shield were very close. Reggie darted sideways out of the crack and grabbed the golden shield. Kerberos slowly turned to face him again. Reggie held up the shield and caught a beam of light, directing it straight into the eyes of Kerberos's middle head. When one of the other heads made a move towards Reggie, he shifted the angle of the shield to blind that one with the light instead. He moved his way around the cavern, shifting the light between heads and occasionally darting back into a crack until Kerberos lost interest. Finally, he reached the skeleton that held the harp-guitar-thingie. He was going to have to drop the shield to grab it. He stared at the sharp teeth of the dog's three heads, dripping with saliva, and gulped. What else could he do?

He dropped the shield.

He grabbed the instrument.

He felt the hot, stinky breath of Kerberos's heads drawing closer.

He quickly strummed the strange instrument. He could play it! But what? Maybe ... "Tune for 'Wild Thing'," Reggie said. He strummed again. The command had worked! He started to sing the old song his guitar teacher loved.

The notes resounded throughout the silent cavern and Reggie looked up to see Kerberos sitting like an obedient puppy, wagging its tail. Reggie sighed with relief and made his way to the tunnel, strumming as he went. Reggie wasn't sure if Kerberos was following him, but he had remembered the other part of what the tall woman had said as well. *Don't look back*. So, he didn't. Even when he could sense the creature was behind him or when the breath from its three heads was so hot on his neck he was sure he was about to be eaten, Reggie kept his eyes straight ahead.

Once out of the tunnel Reggie turned around. Kerberos was still there and was as calm and quiet as a guide dog. The words *Level Complete* popped up before him with dramatic music and Reggie relaxed for a second, and slung the harp over his back.

Chapter 8

The Hind and the Hydra

"Map," said Reggie. When it appeared, it had two letters on it. A capital *I*, currently at the Portal to the Underworld, and a capital *H*, currently moving between two other locations. The *I* was obviously him and the *H* had to be Oliver, which meant Oliver was already on his way to completing another labour while Reggie was just looking at the map.

Reggie noticed that the locations he had been to, and the one Oliver was moving away from, now had a tick beside them.

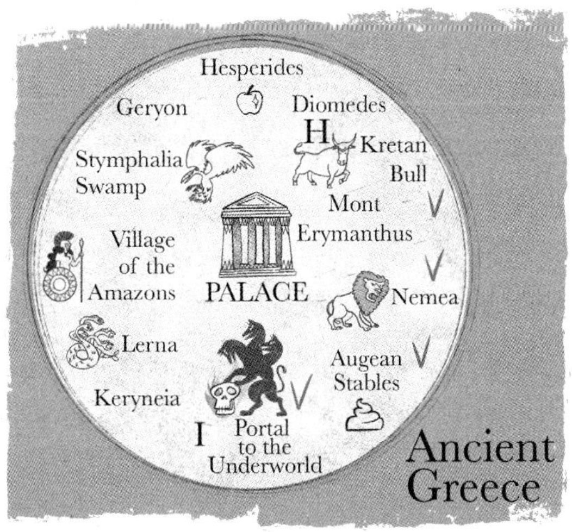

Reggie realised the locations must be ticked once the levels were complete. He watched as the *H* reached its destination; in moments, the location was ticked. How could Oliver have completed a level so quickly? Reggie couldn't let Oliver complete his labours first. There was no time to waste. He had to complete his next task; he had to capture the Keryneian hind.

The Keryneian hind turned out to be an enormous deer with golden antlers. It was far too fast for Reggie to chase down or shoot with his bow and arrow. He scoured the location for anything that might help. Eventually he found a tangled net. By the time he'd finished untangling it, the hind had fallen asleep nearby, so Reggie was able to slip the net over the creature with ease.

When Reggie pulled the map up again, he saw Oliver had completed a second task and was on his way to a third at Stymphalia Swamp.

Reggie took off at a run to his next location, Lerna, to defeat the hydra, whatever that was.

He arrived at an enormous lake. When nothing immediately appeared, he began searching for any useful items or clues. All he found was a burnt-out campfire and a curved, bladed weapon tangled in some grass. While he was pulling it free, he heard a gurgling noise behind him. Reggie turned and saw bubbles on the lake's surface moving towards the shore.

When the bubbles reached the edge of the lake, a snake slithered out of the water. It was no ordinary snake. It was as long as a giraffe is tall and as thick as a tree trunk. It reared up, towering over Reggie. A cold shiver ran down Reggie's spine as it revealed a pair of long, curved fangs.

Reggie wasted no time. He darted forward, slicing through the air with the curved blade and cutting off the hydra's head.

Reggie awaited the triumphant music that accompanied the *Level Complete* announcement, but it didn't come. The headless body of the snake began writhing in the sand like a worm that had been cut in half. Its headless body reared up again and two new heads grew out of its stump where Reggie had cut off the original head.

One of the heads lunged at him. He dodged sideways, but the other head was waiting for him. It dived down, tearing through Reggie's tunic with its fangs and slicing into his skin as well. It stung so badly Reggie dropped to one knee. The head would have gotten him again, but he gathered himself and rolled out of the way just in time. He staggered to his feet and ran. He ran as fast as he could.

Chapter 9

The Birds

"Palace," Reggie stammered as soon as he was out of reach of the hydra. Suddenly, he was standing before King Eurystheus once again. He fell to his knees, clutching his throbbing arm. A purple web of poison spiralled out from where the hydra's fang had got him.

"I need a potion," Reggie said. "Or an antidote or whatever healing methods you have in this game." He really, really hoped there was one.

"Of course," said the king. He waved his hand over Reggie's body. Reggie's pain began to fade. The purple poison vanished. Even the scratches from the Nemean lion healed.

Reggie went from feeling the worst he'd ever felt to the best. But he still had the problem of how to defeat the hydra. He couldn't risk going back to the lake until he'd figured it out.

Reggie pulled out his list of labours. The next one was to retrieve the belt of Hippolyte, Queen of the Amazons. He called up the map. The village of the Amazons was located right beside Stymphalia swamp. Oliver was still there. None of the other labours had taken Oliver this long. Good, Reggie thought, he's finally been stumped. But then he had another thought. What if Oliver was hurt? What if he was as hurt as Reggie had just been and didn't know how to heal himself, or even that he could? And what if Oliver hadn't realised that when you get hurt in this game you get hurt in real life because Reggie had kept that important bit of information to himself?

Reggie's stomach twisted. It wasn't much of a detour to check what was happening at the swamp.

It didn't take Reggie long to get to the swamp. As Reggie approached it, he was deafened by the screeching of birds. In the distance he could see Oliver waist-deep in a bog. He was waving his club in the air, fending off hundreds of birds as they swooped at him.

Whenever the birds got past the club, they pecked at him. As Reggie drew closer, he could see dots of blood all over Oliver's bare arms where the birds had got him. Reggie winced at the thought of what Oliver must be feeling.

"Oliver!" Reggie yelled across the swamp.

Oliver turned, distracted by Reggie's call, and a bird got past his club. It tore off a tiny piece of skin and ate it. Oliver let out a roar of pain and swung the club wildly at the bird. The movement caused him to sink a little deeper into the bog.

"I'm stuck!" Oliver called out, keeping his eyes on the birds. "This big body was too heavy to walk across."

"What's the labour?" Reggie asked.

"To get rid of the birds," Oliver quickly replied. "They're eating me, Reggie! I can feel it! Why can I feel it if it's just a game?"

Reggie's face burned. He shook his head to clear it. He had to get Oliver out of that bog first. He could worry about his guilt later.

A few birds took off from nearby trees and flew towards Oliver. Reggie fired at them with his arrows and was surprised to see the arrows hit their targets and the birds fall from the sky. Finally, this bow was good for something.

He looked around and saw a thick, rope-like vine hanging from one of the trees near Oliver.

Reggie trod carefully into the swamp towards the tree. The ground was soft, but not soft enough for his light body to sink into.

Occasionally a bird took off towards him or Oliver, and he was able to take it down with his bow. He reached the vine and tugged one end of it loose from the tree, sending several birds off into the sky. He took them down as well. Then, bringing the loose end of the vine with him, Reggie stepped out onto the bog towards Oliver. Each step grew softer and softer, though he never sank deeper than his ankles. Being the small sidekick had some benefits after all.

"Take this," Reggie said when he reached Oliver. "Use it to pull yourself out." Up close, he could now see how many peck-wounds Oliver had suffered. It was horrible.

They made it back to solid ground, Oliver dragging himself out with the vine and Reggie firing at any birds that came their way.

"What now?" asked Oliver. "There are still so many birds; you can't shoot them all."

"Maybe I don't need to. You said the labour was to get rid of the birds, not kill them," Reggie said. "What were you trying to do out in that bog?"

"I thought I could scare them. There was a big shield out there and I was banging my club on it. It was working, but then I hit too hard, and it sank. When I tried to run, I sank too."

"It sounds like you had the right idea. Maybe instead of scaring them away, we can lure them away."

Reggie pulled out the strange musical instrument from the cavern, which he'd hung across his back. "I got this at one of the labours."

"A harp!" Oliver said.

"Um, yeah. I was able to tame this massive three-headed dog with it. Maybe it'll work here, too."

As soon as Reggie played the first notes, the birds took to the sky. They flew towards him but didn't attack. Instead, the birds hovered above Reggie in a black cloud, ferociously flapping their wings.

Just as he had with Kerberos, Reggie kept walking, continually strumming the instrument. The birds followed. He and Oliver walked away from the swamp together, and as soon as they left the location the birds took off into the sky and flew away. The level was complete.

Reggie turned to Oliver with a grin. But his smile fell at the sight of Oliver's bleeding arms and pale face. "Quick, we need to get back to the palace," Reggie said.

The shortcut worked and, in an instant, the boys were back at the palace. "You need to heal him," Reggie said to the king, struggling to support Oliver's weight. The king waved his hand over Oliver's body. They watched as Oliver's trickling blood was sucked back into the peck wounds and the skin healed over them. "That was amazing," Oliver exclaimed as the colour returned to his cheeks. "How did you figure that out?"

"I got hurt, too. Really badly. I returned to the palace after escaping the hydra; the king healed me. I might not still be here otherwise."

"Lucky it's just a game," Oliver laughed with relief.

Reggie looked at his feet. "Oliver, there's something I have to tell you."

"Yes?" Oliver said, frowning.

"I think ... I think when we're hurt in this game, we're hurt in real life. That's why it feels so real. It *is* real."

"Are you saying we could have died back there?"

"I think so."

"I can't believe it! That's wild! How long have you known about this?"

Reggie's stomach was in knots. "Since the Nemean lion."

"What?" Oliver looked furious. "Why didn't you tell me?"

"I'm sorry. I should have. I was mad, and maybe a bit jealous you were doing so well at the game. It's just that you do so well at everything.

Oliver's expression softened. "I get it. I feel the same way about you sometimes."

Reggie looked up, surprised. "No way."

Oliver snorted. "I think maybe we just need to get over it. We're both good at different stuff. That's probably why it's easier to complete these labours together."

Reggie nodded. "I think you're right."

"So how about we finish this thing together? But no more secrets and no more jealousy."

"Deal," Reggie said. "No more secrets and no more jealousy."

Chapter 10

Return to the Hydra

Oliver and Reggie completed the next three tasks together. They stole the cattle of Geryon the giant by herding the animals backwards so that their tracks couldn't be followed. They retrieved the golden apples of the Hesperides, daughters of the gods, by convincing the snake that guarded them to check that no other fruit in the garden was being stolen. And they obtained the belt of Hippolyte, Queen of the Amazon warriors, simply because she liked Oliver's, or rather Herakles's, smile and just gave it to them. Reggie didn't let that one bother him.

After that, all that remained was to go back and defeat the hydra. Reggie shuddered at the thought.

Reggie and Oliver approached the sandy shore of the lake together. The hydra must have returned to the water because it was nowhere to be seen.

Reggie still had the curved blade but went to check for anything else that might be useful. Oliver squatted over the burnt-out campfire. "There's flint here," he called out to Reggie. "And plenty of firewood. Maybe we're meant to make a fire."

Reggie turned to look at Oliver when something caught his eye. "Whatever you're going to do, I'd do it fast," Reggie said, pointing to the water. Bubbles had appeared on the lake's surface and were slowly moving towards the shore.

Oliver quickly stacked the firewood and began using the flint to try to create a spark. After three failed attempts, the kindling caught alight, and, faster than any campfire in real life, there was a raging fire burning.

Then the hydra emerged, still with the two heads it had grown when Reggie last encountered it.

"What now?" Reggie yelled, holding the curved blade ready.

Oliver glanced at the fire. "I don't know." He drew his sword.

One head went for Reggie and he dodged out of the way towards the fire. Oliver sliced with his sword, cutting off one head, then quickly dodging the other. The stump left after the head had been cut off fell limp, while the remaining head flailed around wildly. Then, just as had happened last time, two heads grew in place of the one that had been cut off. Reggie's stomach dropped. The hydra now had three heads. He was about to yell at Oliver to run when he looked down at the fire. A long, narrow log had rolled partially into the flames, so only one end was alight. Reggie grabbed it and held it up like the Olympic torch.

"What are you doing?" Oliver yelled. One of the hydra heads dived at Oliver. Reggie ran towards it, slicing off the head with the curved blade. Then, before it could sprout another two heads in its place, he plunged the burning stick onto the stump.

The boys didn't have time to wait to see if Reggie's idea had worked. Oliver spun around and sliced off the second head. While dodging the third head, Reggie darted forward and burnt that stump as well. Together they sliced off the third head and Reggie burnt its stump triumphantly.

The headless serpent lay in the sand. Reggie and Oliver backed away, waiting for it to wriggle back to life, but it didn't. With a sigh of relief, Reggie heard the dramatic music and saw *Level Complete* appear above the hydra's body.

Suddenly Reggie and Oliver were standing back at the palace in front of King Eurystheus.

The king stood and raised his hands. “You have completed all twelve labours of Herakles.”

“Can we go? Can we leave now?” Oliver asked, clutching his wounded shoulder.

“Wait, wait,” Reggie said. “Heal us first.”

The king waved his hand over them. “I have healed you of all your wounds. Now you may return whence you came.”

Reggie’s vision blurred. He began to see the real world layered on top of this one. His body tingled and then he was standing right back where he had been when he was sucked into the game, as if nothing had ever happened.

Chapter 11

Back at Last

Oliver and Reggie were back in the Cognitivia Games office. Reggie looked down at his own body. He touched his arms, legs and chest. He felt his face; it was definitely his, not a bit of facial hair to be found. He looked at Oliver and grinned. They were back. Reggie and Oliver were so relieved and happy, they even hugged. Then they realised Mr Nguyen, Becky and the two developers who had left earlier were standing there staring at them.

Mr Nguyen gave them the look that said, *I'll deal with you two later and you're really not going to like it*. Reggie imagined rubbish collection for weeks on end. Mr Nguyen marched them out of the room to where the rest of the class waited.

"What time is it?" Oliver asked.

"Lunchtime!" one of their classmates said.

If it was only lunchtime the game mustn't have taken as long to complete as it had felt like.

As the class walked to a nearby park to have their lunch, Reggie and Oliver hung back.

"That was wild," Oliver said. "I don't think I'll

ever want to play another video game again."

"Are you joking?" Reggie said. "It was amazing! Sure, they have to fix a few bugs but ... wow! I wonder if I could get an internship here."

"It's all yours," Oliver laughed. "I'll stick with my books. Maybe read up on some more Greek myths. You know, just in case I'm ever sucked into another life-threatening video game."

"Good plan," Reggie said. "You were certainly the perfect person to get stuck with." He kicked the pavement, looking at his feet. "I couldn't have gotten out of there without you."

Oliver smiled. "Thanks. I definitely couldn't have done it without you either."

They both grinned. Reggie wasn't sure how getting stuck in a video game together had changed things, but he knew he wasn't going to dread the carpool to school any more.